Resonance

A Multicultural Cello Method

Book 1

Hilary Glen, D.M.A.
Laura Usiskin, D.M.A.
Angelique Montes, D.M.A.
Bianca d'Avila do Prado, M.M.
Jennifer Carpenter, D.M.A.

ACCESS KEY: RMCM#DuPre1

Resonance Music, LLC
www.resonancemcm.com

Copyright © 2025 Resonance
All Rights Reserved.

Any duplication, adaptation, or compilation of this composition and arrangement requires written consent of the author(s).
Unauthorized uses are an infringement of the U.S. Copyright Act and are punishable by law.

About Resonance

Resonance: A Multicultural Cello Method is a pedagogical approach to learning the cello using music that has contributed to American culture. We have included pieces and musical elements from a variety of backgrounds, cultures, and time periods with the goal of creating relevancy and belonging for anyone wanting to learn the instrument. Through this method, students learn to play the cello using music that is representative of themselves, their heritage, and the cultures around them. We aim to instill foundational cello techniques while also offering this method as a stepping stone towards achieving greater musical inclusivity.

Note to Teachers

Thank you for using this book! The pieces are organized in a suggested sequential order, though we invite teachers to use this book in the way that best fits their pedagogical approach. We have included preparatory exercises that isolate new skills and highlight tricky spots worth drilling, emphasizing key techniques that we find are essential to building a well-rounded cellist.

We encourage you to visit our website for additional resources, including recordings, song lyrics, and further cultural context, all available at www.resonancemcm.com. Access to the recordings is included with your purchase of this book. Enter the Access Key found in the front of your book.

Acknowledgments

The Resonance Method Team extends its heartfelt gratitude to the many people and organizations who offered feedback, advice, and financial support to make this book possible. We would like to give special thanks to Lisa Husseini for her indispensable counsel and to Melanie Zeck at the Library of Congress for her cultural guidance. *Resonance: A Multicultural Cello Method* is supported in part by an alumni grant and mentorship from the New World Symphony BLUE (Build, Learn, Understand, Experiment) program, which empowers the NWS network of artistic entrepreneurs to redefine the future of classical music through inclusive community and equity-focused initiatives. NWS BLUE projects are made possible with support from the Maxine and Stuart Frankel Foundation and NWS's Fund for New Ventures. This book has also received grant support from Eastman's Institute for Music Leadership's funds from the Paul R. Judy Center for Innovation and Research. We are grateful to esteemed pedagogues Pam Devenport and Avi Friedlander for their helpful feedback on earlier drafts of the book and to David Dunford for creating the piano accompaniments. We also acknowledge the following individuals who supported Resonance Method's vision through generous financial donations: Andrew Dunn, Jeremy Glen and Melissa Colangelo, Jim Glen and Connie Cook Glen, Heather Hadley, Kathleen Kemp, Daniel Ketter, Karen Morris, Shaianne Osterreich and Reuben Peeters, and Zachary Sweet.

Contents

5   Before Dinner: Version 1

6   Duerme, Mi Tesoro • Sleep, My Treasure

6   Before Dinner: Version 2

7   Dhobi Aaya • The Washerman

8   Dodo ti pitit manman • Sleep Mommy's Little One

9   Pezinho • Little Foot

10   Alwardat Albayda • The White Rose

11   Escravos de Jó • Slaves of Job

12   *Chamamé* from Enchelación

13   Sakura • Cherry Blossom

14   Mòlìhuā • Jasmine Flower

15   Arirang • Beloved One

16   Swing Low, Sweet Chariot

Before Dinner: Version 1

Before Dinner is a song from the Democratic Republic of Congo. The lyrics describe preparing for dinnertime. It uses call-and-response, a popular musical technique with origins from Sub-Saharan African traditions.

Congolese Folk Song

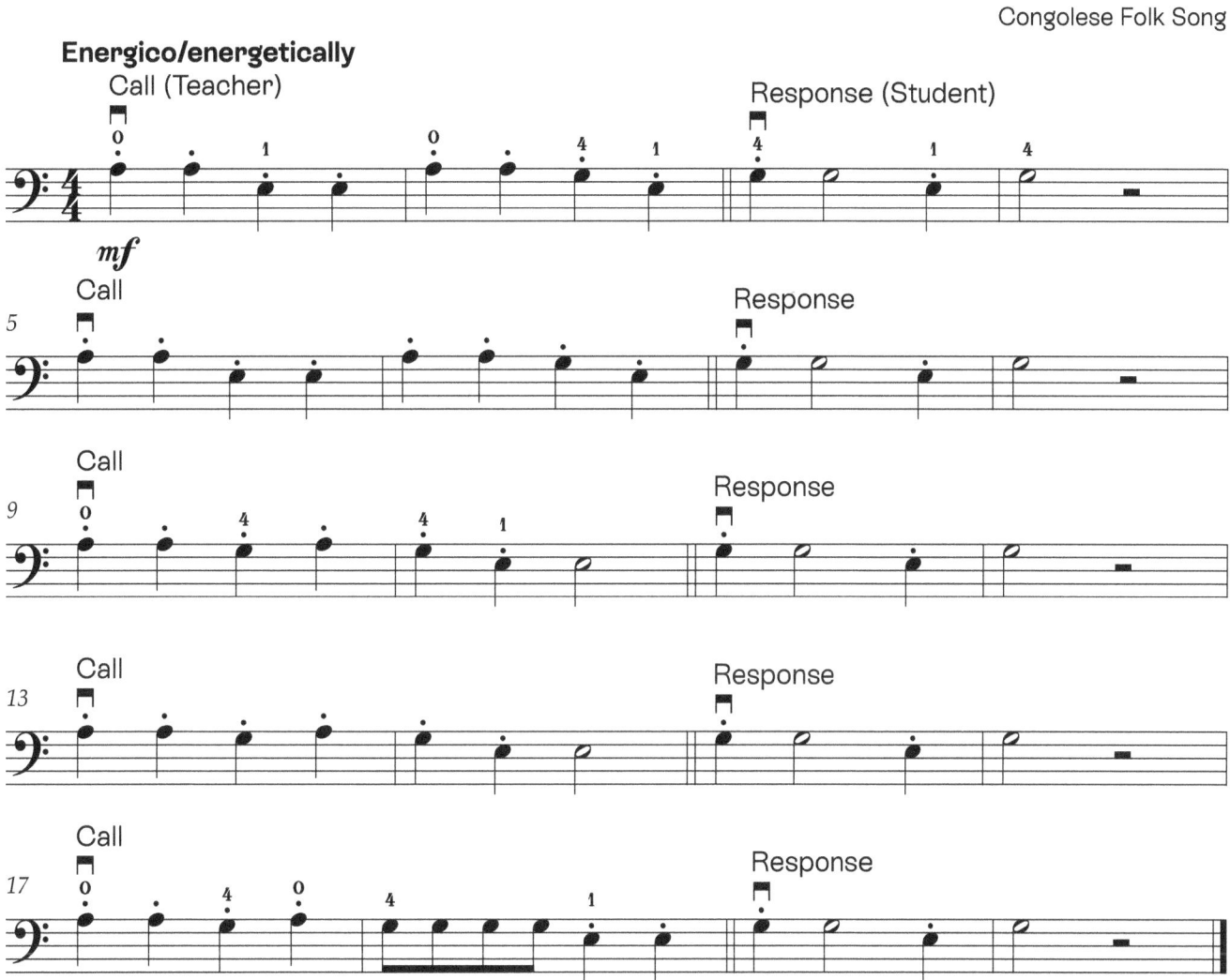

Duerme, Mi Tesoro • Sleep, My Treasure

Duerme, Mi Tesoro /DWER-me mee te-SOH-roh/ is a Puerto Rican lullaby. Lullabies are songs sung to children to help them fall asleep. The lyrics encourage the child to sleep well, saying that little angels will be watching over them.

Puerto Rican Folk Song

Dolce/sweetly

Before Dinner: Version 2

Congolese Folk Song

Energico/energetically

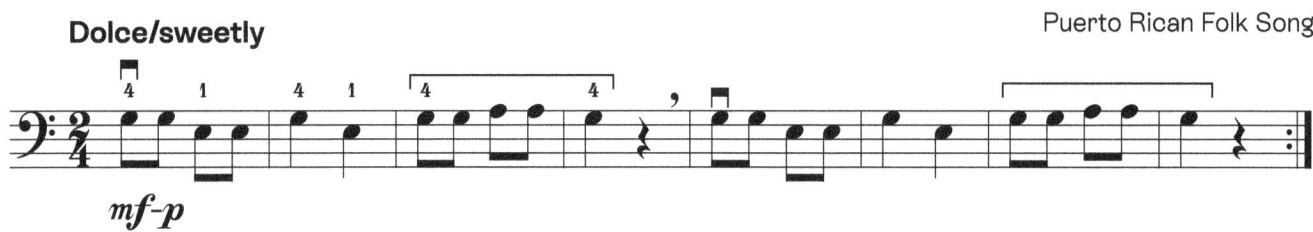

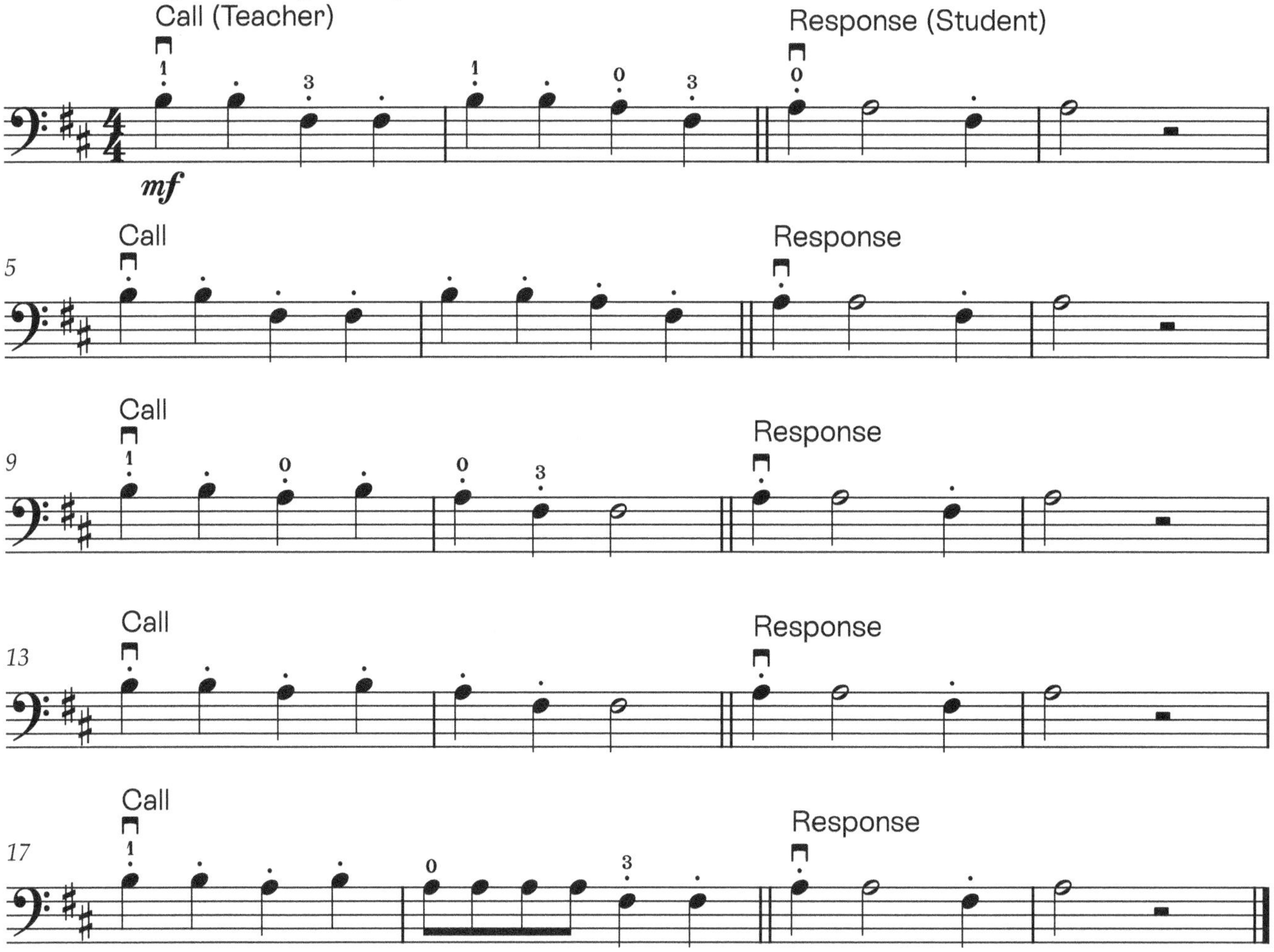

Dhobi Aaya • The Washerman

धोबी आया

Dhobi Aaya /DOH-bee AHY-uh/ is a popular Hindi children's counting song. The lyrics illustrate a washerman counting out ten pieces of laundry. The stomping in this version aligns with the counting portion of the song.

Preparation

Dhobi Aaya

Hindi Folk Song

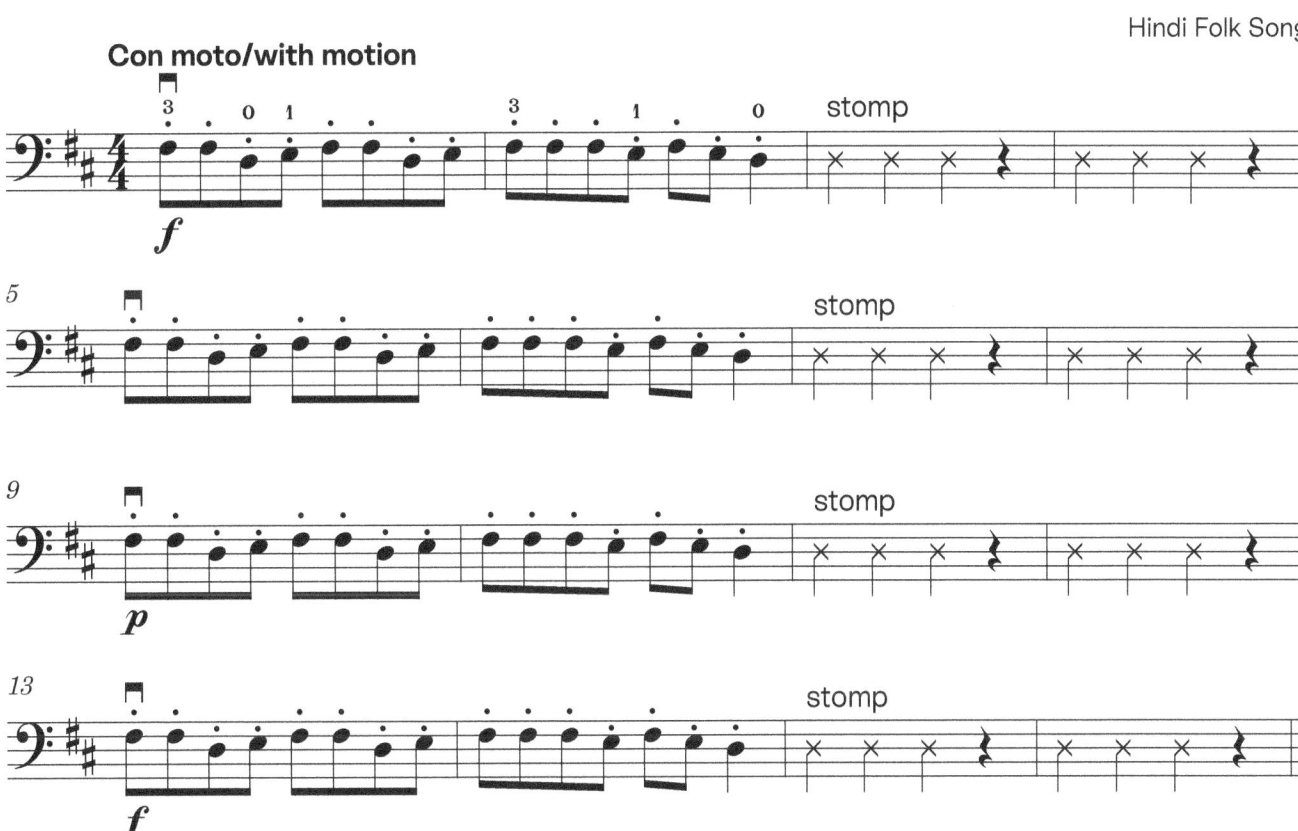

Dodo ti pitit manman • Sleep Mommy's Little One

Dodo ti pitit manman /DOE-doe TEE pee-TEET muh-MUH/ is a popular Haitian lullaby. The lyrics jokingly warn the little one of being eaten by a crab if they don't fall asleep, but - fortunately - the sweet melody succeeds in lulling the little one to sleep.

Preparations

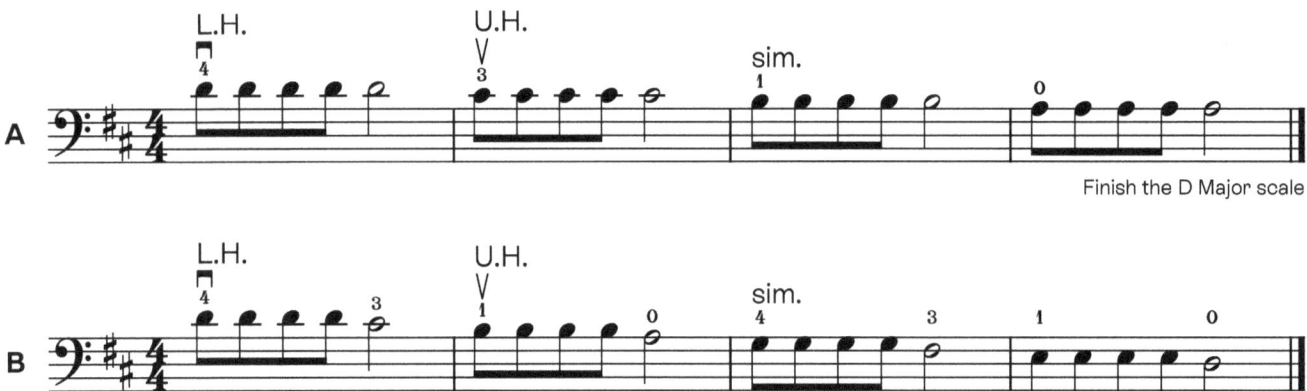

Finish the D Major scale

Drill Spot

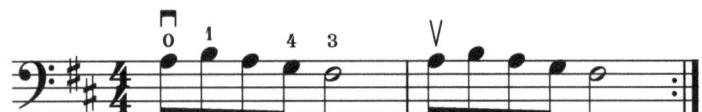

Dodo ti pitit manman

Haitian Folk Song

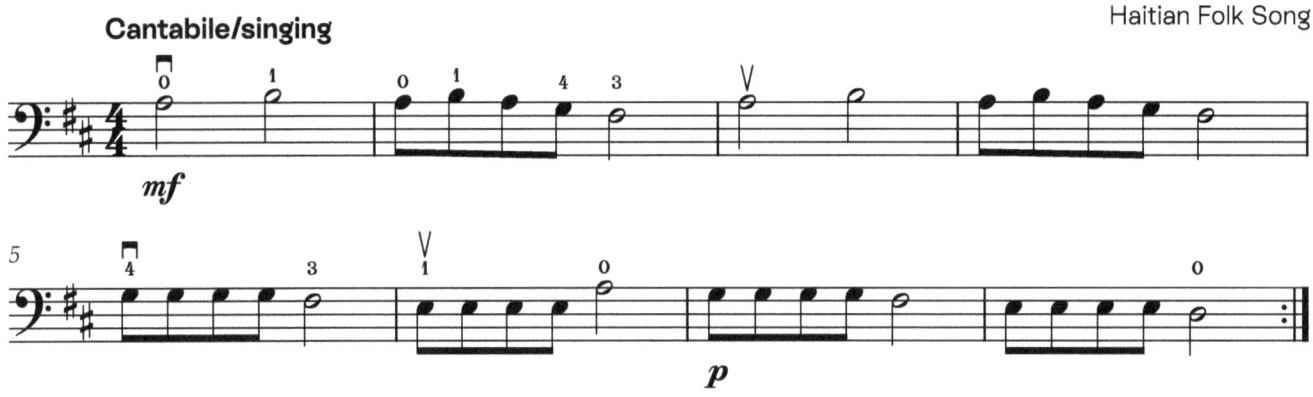

Pezinho • Little Foot

Pezinho /pez-EEN-yoh/ is a nursery rhyme that came to southern Brazil with the immigrants from Açores Island. A staple of Gaúcha culture, *Pezinho* is both a song and dance that children in Rio Grande do Sul learn at a very early age. Special celebrations feature children and adults dancing to *Pezinho* while dressed in traditional attire.

Preparation

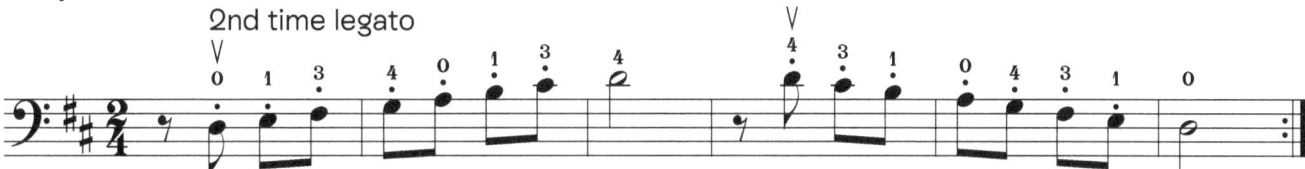

Drill Spots

The lyrics of the song describe dance steps. Visit our website to learn the dance!

Pezinho

Brazilian Folk Song

Alwardat Albayda • The White Rose

الوردة البيضاء

Alwardat Albayda /ahl-WAHR-daht ahl-BAY-dah/ is an Iraqi song sung by school children in Arabic. It uses the natural minor scale.

Preparation

Alwardat Albayda

Iraqi Folk Song

Escravos de Jó • Slaves of Job

Escravos de Jó /es-KRAV-ohs de HO/ is a well-known circle game played in all regions of Brazil. Enslaved people used to sing this song in their celebrations while dancing and playing games following the music. This song was prohibited during the slavery period in Brazil but survived and was passed on aurally through generations. To this day, children across the country sing and play games to *Escravos de Jó*.

Preparation

Escravos de Jó

Brazilian Folk Song

Visit www.resonancemcm.com for additional resources for all the pieces, including recordings, song lyrics, and further cultural context.

Chamamé

Chamamé /CHA-mah-mey/ is the first movement of *Enchelación* /en-chey-lah-see-OHN/. This piece was composed in 2019 by Argentinian composer, cellist, and teacher Fernando Manuel Dieguez. Originally for cello ensemble, Enchelación consists of four movements that each feature a different Latin American rhythm. While the Chamamé rhythm originally comes from the province of Corrientes in Argentina, it has spread to the south of Brazil, Paraguay, and Uruguay.

Preparations

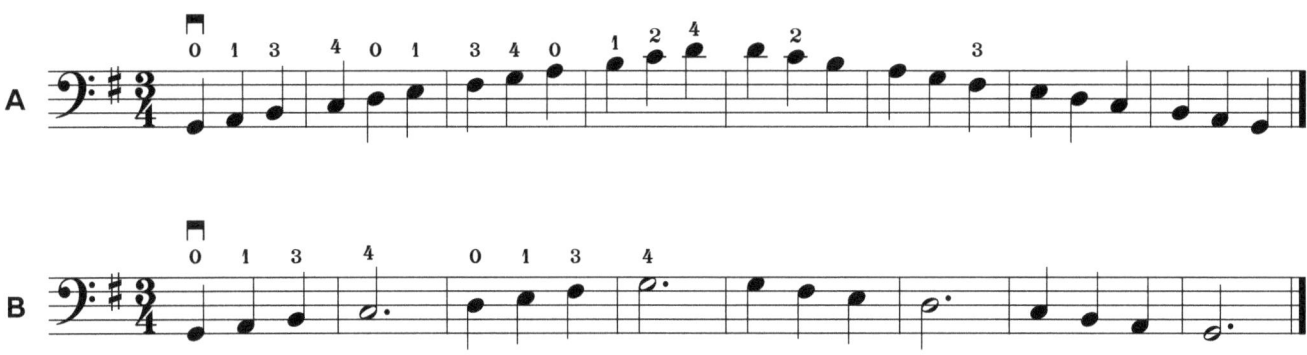

Chamamé

Fernando Manuel Dieguez

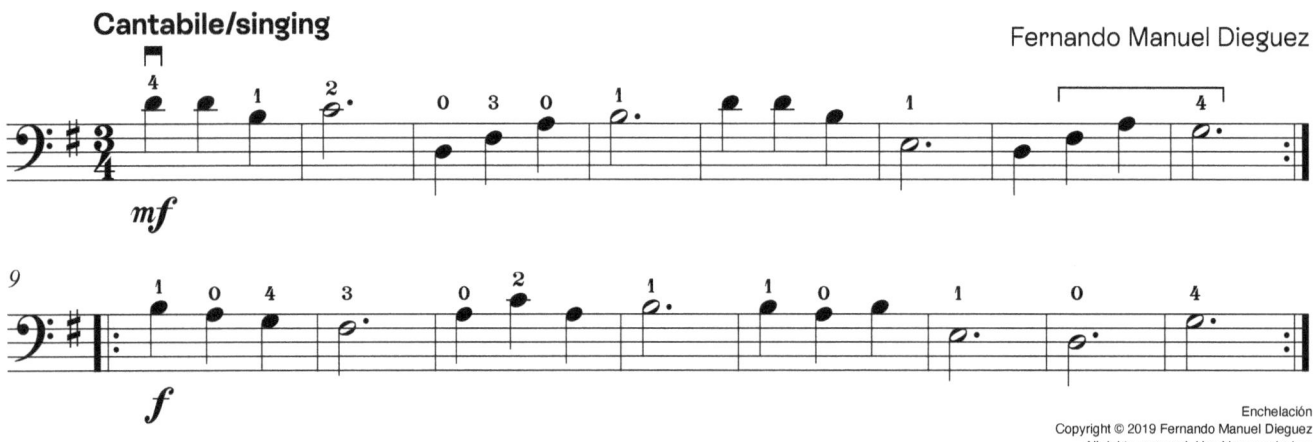

Enchelación
Copyright © 2019 Fernando Manuel Dieguez
All rights reserved. Used by permission.

Sakura • Cherry Blossom

さくら

Sakura /SAH-koo-rah/ is a popular Japanese folk song about springtime and the blooming of the national flower of Japan, the cherry blossom. The melody most likely originated during the Edo era (1603-1868), while the lyrics were added in the Meiji Era (1868-1912). The song uses the pentatonic (five-note) scale E-F-A-B-C.

Preparation

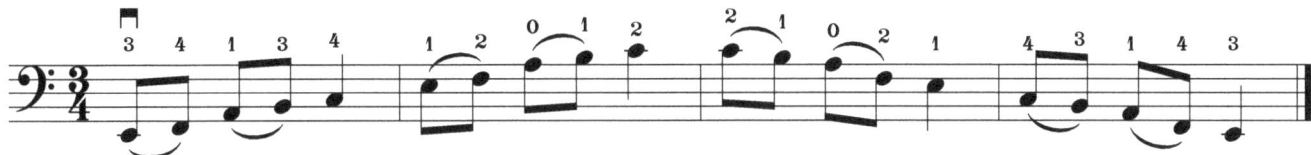

Drill Spot

Sakura

Japanese Folk Song

Mòlìhuā • Jasmine Flower

茉莉花

Mòlìhuā /moa-lee-hoaah/ is a Chinese song that has existed for centuries. It was one of the first Chinese folk songs to be known outside of China. It uses the pentatonic scale D-E-F♯-A-B.

Preparation

Mòlìhuā

Chinese Folk Song

Arirang • Beloved One

아리랑

Arirang /ah-ree-rahng/ is a celebrated Korean folk song. People from both northern and southern regions of Korea are known to sing it as a symbol of unity. Linguistic experts believe that "arirang" can translate to mean "beloved one" in ancient Korean. The song is based upon the pentatonic scale D-E-G-A-B.

Preparation

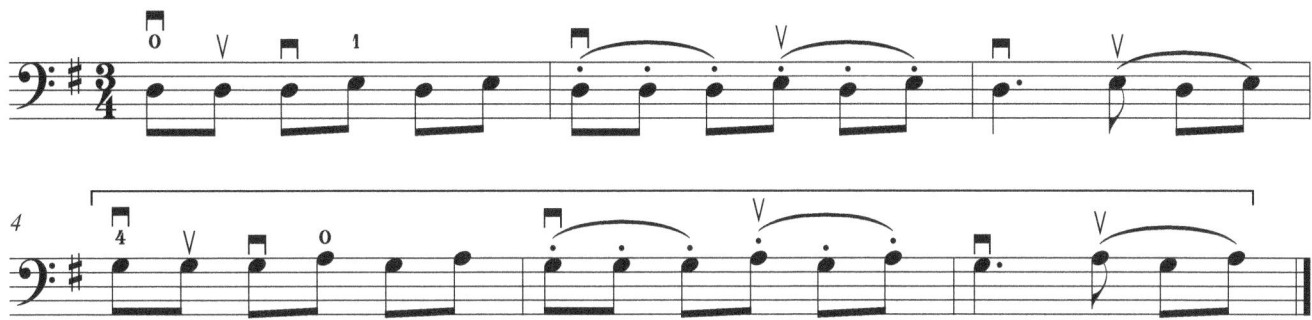

Arirang

Korean Folk Song

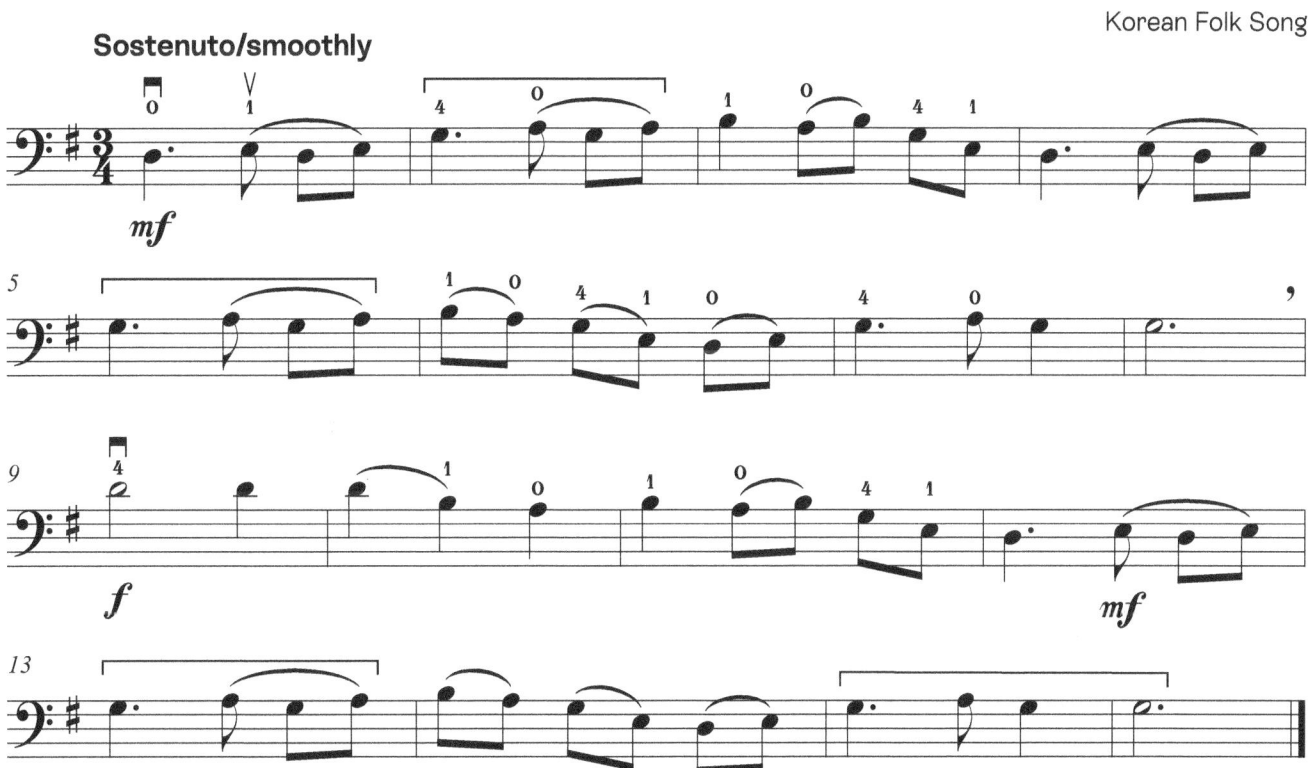

Swing Low, Sweet Chariot

Swing Low, Sweet Chariot is a well-known, African-American spiritual. Its original form uses call-and-response, drawing from Sub-Saharan African musical traditions. A leader sings the differentiated lines, and the choir replies, "Comin' for to carry me home."

Preparation

Drill Spot

Swing Low, Sweet Chariot

African-American Spiritual

Symbols

Here are the pedagogical symbols used in this book:

’	Bow retake, resulting in two down-bows in a row
⌐ ¬	Left-hand fingers down, making a tunnel
L.H.	Lower half of the bow
U.H.	Upper half of the bow

Visit www.resonancemcm.com for additional resources for all the pieces, including recordings, song lyrics, and further cultural context.

www.ingramcontent.com/pod-product-compliance
Lightning Source LLC
Chambersburg PA
CBHW040008080526
44586CB00027B/2923